discovermore

The Lives of Animals

Animal Camouflage

Doug Bradley

Britannica
Educational Publishing
IN ASSOCIATION WITH
THE ROSEN PUBLISHING GROUP

Published in 2024 by Britannica Educational Publishing (a trademark of Encyclopædia Britannica, Inc.) in association with The Rosen Publishing Group, Inc.
2544 Clinton Street, Buffalo, NY 14224

Distributed exclusively by Rosen Publishing.
To see additional Britannica Educational Publishing titles, go to rosenpublishing.com.

Editor: Dwayne Hicks
Book Design: Michael Flynn

Photo Credits: Cover Baishev/Shutterstock.com; (series background) Dai Yim/Shutterstock.com; p. 4 Mark Brandon/Shutterstock.com; p. 5 Rudmer Zwerver/Shutterstock.com; p. 6 Wright Out There/Shutterstock.com; p. 7 Cigdem Cooper/Shutterstock.com; p. 8 Grigorev Mikhail/Shutterstock.com; p. 9 Milan Zygmunt/Shutterstock.com; p. 11 (top) Wilm Ihlenfeld/Shutterstock.com; p. 11 (bottom) Port_Folio/Shutterstock.com; p. 12 Arunee Rodloy/Shutterstock.com; p. 13 Ethan Daniels/Shutterstock.com; p. 14 Chantal de Bruijne/Shutterstock.com; p. 15 David A Litman/Shutterstock.com; p. 16 Jan Hejda/Shutterstock.com; p. 17 Gosza Wlodarczyk/Shutterstock.com; p. 18 Mark_Kostich/Shutterstock.com; p. 19 Sista Vongjintanaruks/Shutterstock.com; p. 21 (top) Rich Carey/Shutterstock.com; p. 21 (bottom) Silvia Pascual/Shutterstock.com; p. 22 WWWoronin/Shutterstock.com; p. 23 3dsam79/Shutterstock.com; p. 24 Danita Delimont/Shutterstock.com; p. 25 Jamikorn Sooktaramorn/Shutterstock.com; p. 26 CHAINFOTO24/Shutterstock.com; p. 27 Dirk Ercken/Shutterstock.com; p. 28 Keith Hider/Shutterstock.com; p. 29 Divelvanov/Shutterstock.com.

Cataloging-in-Publication Data

Names: Bradley, Doug, 1971-.
Title: Animal camouflage / Doug Bradley.
Description: New York : Britannica Educational Publishing, in Association with Rosen Educational Services. 2024. | Series: Discover more: the lives of animals | Includes glossary and index.
Identifiers: ISBN 9781642828603 (library bound) | ISBN 9781642828597 (pbk) | ISBN 9781642828610 (ebook)
Subjects: LCSH: Camouflage (Biology)--Juvenile literature. | Protective coloration (Biology)--Juvenile literature. | Animals--Color--Juvenile literature. | Animal behavior--Juvenile literature.
Classification: LCC QL767.B683 2024 | DDC 591.47′2–dc23

Manufactured in the United States of America

CPSIA Compliance Information: Batch #CSBRIT24. For further information contact Rosen Publishing at 1-800-237-9932.

Contents

Defining Camouflage

Have you ever wondered how an animal might protect themselves from being hurt? One of the main ways is camouflage. Camouflage is coloring or patterns that help disguise an animal. This is useful to animals in many ways, and there are many different types of camouflage. Most types help animals blend into their **habitats**. This allows animals to hide or defend themselves from animals that might eat them.

The walking stick, for instance, is an insect that looks a lot like a long stick or a twig. A hungry animal won't notice the walking stick because it blends into its surroundings, so the insect won't be eaten.

The walking stick looks like it's a part of the tree.

A lynx blends in with its surroundings as it searches for its next meal.

Camouflage can also be used by an animal on the hunt for food. Big cats have patterned coats that help them to hide from their prey. A lion's light-colored coat blends in perfectly with dry grasslands. Changing or matching colors is used by prey and predators alike.

WORD WISE

Habitats are the natural homes of an animal, plant, or other living things. Habitats include deserts, rain forests, and more.

Hidden in Plain Sight

Tawny frogmouths are excellent at disguising themselves. These birds have brown and black feathers that help them to blend into the trees where they live. They sit on a tree branch, close their yellow eyes, and tilt their heads back. They sometimes wait in the tree, motionless, for prey to pass by. This method of camouflage is known as background matching.

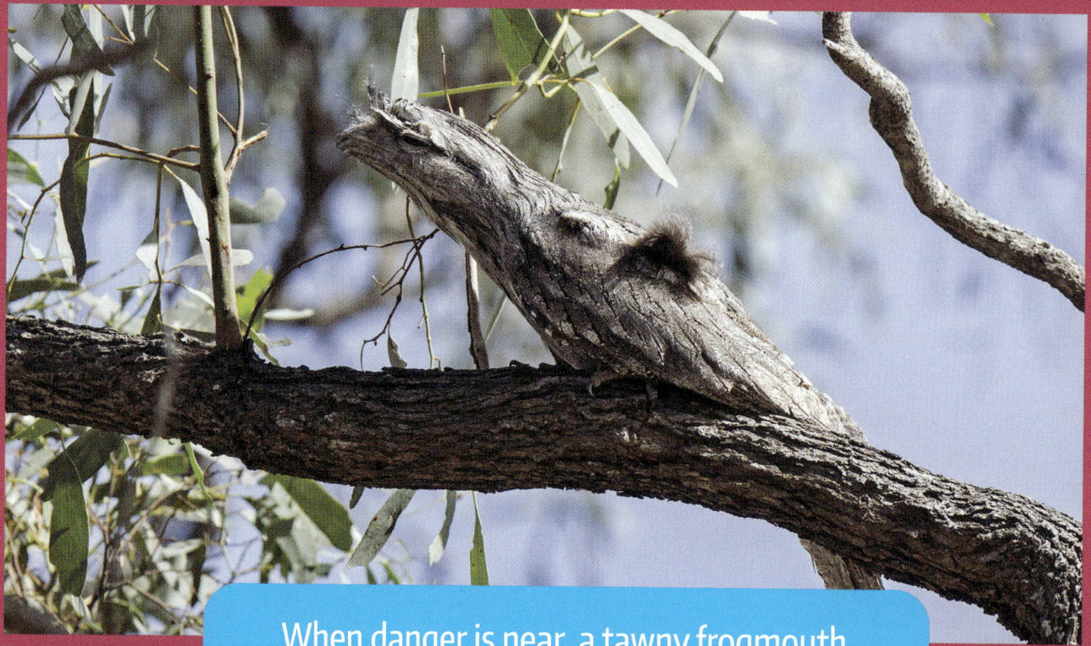

When danger is near, a tawny frogmouth straightens its back to look just like a branch.

Even baby stonefish are excellent at camouflage.

Living well underneath the ocean's surface, among rocks and coral reefs, are the most venomous fish on Earth: stonefish. Stonefish blend in almost exactly with their surroundings in both texture and color. They wait for shrimp or small fish to swim by. Then they open their mouths for a quick meal. They protect themselves from predators with their 13 sharp spines and venomous sacs.

Consider This

What other animals can change the color of their skin to match their surroundings? If you look carefully, you will find more in this book!

Background matching can even be done by animals without color. For example, flatfish larva allow light to pass through their transparent bodies, allowing them to hide in plain sight. Herring also have an interesting way of matching their background. Their silvery scales reflect the things around them like a mirror, making it seem as if they disappeared into thin air.

The ghost glass catfish has a transparent body. You can see directly through its body!

The green algae on the sloth's fur matches the surrounding leaves, allowing the sloth to blend in with its surroundings.

Certain animals receive camouflage assistance from other organisms. The slow-moving sloth has a thick coat that is a perfect habitat for different types of algae. Algae are plantlike organisms. These algae are blue-green in the wet season and brown in the dry season. The sloth becomes camouflaged among the trees as its coat becomes covered by the growing algae.

Color Modification

Some animals can camouflage themselves by altering the texture of their skin. Both the color and the surface of the skin may change.

Organisms on land and in the water can change their colors. Flounder can change color to match the sand at the bottom of the ocean. Broadclub cuttlefish have skin cells that can change to match the rocks and coral reefs where they live. This keeps them safe from most predators and helps them to sneak up on smaller fish.

Some people think chameleons change colors to blend into their surroundings. In fact, color can change based on temperature, light, and emotions. The changing of a chameleon's color can also be used to communicate with other chameleons.

The texture of the moth's body matches the tree bark perfectly.

compare and contrast

How does camouflage work differently for animals that are prey and animals that are predators?

The chameleon's skin changed to match the leaves, as it waits for an insect to fly by for dinner.

An animal's color can change with the seasons. In the winter, the fur of the snowshoe hare turns white to match its snowy environment. This keeps the hare hidden from predators. When the snow melts, the hare's fur turns brown. Decorator crabs can match their backgrounds perfectly because they use the things around them. They are able to attach seaweed, algae, and ocean rubble to their shells, making it easy for them to hide.

The decorator crab lives up to its name, as it adorns itself with the colors of the rock.

Consider This

How does an animal's surroundings effect the color changes of their skin or fur?

Although it has eight large legs, the day octopus slithers around while mimicking the colors beneath it to hide.

Animals are born with the ability to change color. The day octopus can change both the color and texture of its skin. This is because of the millions of **pigment** cells it has. The cells grow smaller and larger to match the color of the background and its texture. When hungry sharks or dolphins swim by, the day octopus can mimic, or match, the nearby rocks. This camouflage also helps the octopus hunt. As it looks for crab, shrimp, and snails to eat, the creature disguises itself with the color of the ocean floor.

WORD WISE

Pigment is the coloring material inside of the skin cells of animals.

Optical Illusions

Spots and stripes can be found on the fur of some animals to hide their shape. These patterns trick the eyes, so it is hard for other animals to see them. This is called disruptive coloration. Black-and-white-striped zebras are a perfect example of this. When zebras cluster together, lions have a hard time making out the shape of just one zebra. Their eyes only register a collection of stripes.

A zebra's stripes are like a human's fingerprints--no two are exactly the same.

A group of fish swimming together in **synchrony** is called a school.

Disruptive coloration can also be found underwater. When a predator is near, fish like herring and cod cluster, or gather, together. They face the same way and can change direction at the same time. This helps the fish look like one big animal, which keeps hungry animals away. The predator has a hard time finding only one to eat.

WORD WISE

Synchrony means moving together.

A pattern of spots and stripes make up the skin of a boa constrictor. This design is hard for prey to see the large snake slithering in tall grasses and along tree branches.

Predators use their spots and stripes to hide against the background as they hunt. The pattern of fur on tigers, jaguars, and cheetahs makes them very hard to see. By the time their prey does see them, it's too late.

The darker color of the boa constrictor's skin allows it to move across the tree without being noticed.

Giraffes are the tallest living animal, but their colors help them to hide among the trees. Giraffes are covered with brown spots from their long legs to their long necks. These spots blend in with the colors of the trees and the patterns of shadows in the grasslands where they live. Hungry hyenas, lions, leopards, and African wild dogs have to look hard to find them.

Some types of blenny fish have spots that change as the fish moves, matching the sponges and algae patches that it swims over.

A giraffe's height doesn't just help it to reach tall leaves for food. A giraffe's height also allows it to see oncoming predators from far away.

Consider This

Being tall makes it harder to hide! What are some ways a taller animal might hide itself from other animals?

Copycat Colors

Another type of camouflage is called mimicry, in which animals match the color of another creature.

In some cases, mimicry can trick predators into staying away. The harmless scarlet king snake has markings that make it look like the deadly coral snake. The coral snake is the most toxic snake in the United States. Both snakes have striking red, yellow, and black rings, although their color patterns are different. A coral snake's red rings are next to the yellow rings, but a king snake's red rings are next to the black rings.

A coral snake eats frogs, lizards, and other smaller snakes.

Animals can even have spots on their bodies that look like eyes. The four-eye butterfly fish has a large spot on each side of its body that looks like an eye. The extra "eye" may confuse predators. The elephant hawk-moth caterpillar has four false eyes on top of its body. These false eyes make the caterpillar seem larger than it is, which scares away predators.

Some animals use mimicry to prey on other creatures. The tongue of the alligator snapping turtle looks like a worm. The turtle lies in water with its mouth open, inviting fish to grab the "worm." But as soon as they're inside of the turtle's mouth, it eats them.

Alligator snapping turtles are the largest freshwater turtles in the world.

Did You Know?

Coral snakes are non-aggressive. Less than 1% of snake bites in America are from them.

Contrasting Colors

When the top of an animal's body is darker than its belly, it's called countershading. This is a common camouflage for marine animals. When seen from below, these animals blend in with the lighter surface water. When seen from above, their darker colors blend in with shadows on the ocean floor. This makes it difficult for predators and prey alike to notice the animal.

The countershading on marine animals, like great white sharks, whales, and dolphins, allows them to hide from their prey until they are close enough to eat them. Penguins rely on countershading in two ways. It helps them hunt fish and protect themselves. A penguin's white underbelly is hard to see against the ice in Antarctica, where these birds live. It keeps them hidden from the small fish that they prey on. Countershading also protects the penguins while hiding from predators, such as hungry seals, sea lions, sharks, and killer whales.

Blue whales appear blue when seen from the surface or underwater. They also blend in with the ocean fog, making it difficult for other animals to spot them.

compare and contrast

How does countershading work differently for predators compared to prey?

The South American Humboldt penguin can shoot through the water at speeds of 30 miles (48.3 km) an hour.

Illumination

Certain animals can even create their own light. The light and shadows they create is called counterillumination. Some shallow-water squid use light to blend in with moonlight. The cookie-cutter shark produces light that attracts prey. A black band behind its jaw makes the shark look small. When the prey gets close, the fish twists around for a big bite. Counterillumination is especially important for animals that live in the ocean, where it is very dark.

The angler fish has a fishing rod-like spine on its forehead that sends out light so it can see in the dark ocean.

Lanternfish use bioluminescence to easily see prey and predators.

Chemicals in an animal's body can be used to make light. This is called **bioluminescence**. The deep-sea viperfish has a part that glows and hangs in front of its mouth to draw in prey.

The stoplight loosejaw fish can produce a blue-green light and a red light. The loosejaw can see its prey without being noticed because some fish are unable to see the color red.

WORD WISE

Bioluminescence is the light produced by a chemical reaction within a living thing.

Attractive Colors

Color can also be used by an animal to attract predators and prey in a feature called **alluring** coloration.

The blue-tailed skink lizard uses alluring coloration for its own safety. Its bright blue tail attracts predators to just that part of the body. When a predator grabs its tail, the lizard can easily shed it and dart away with all its important body parts still attached.

Sea stars have many arms that attract fast-moving predators. The sea star can even grow a new arm if one is bitten off by a predator.

Striped skunks are nocturnal creatures, so they use their colors to blend in at night.

Poison dart frogs are only about 0.75 inch (1.9 cm) to 1.5 inches (3.8 cm)—about the same size as a human fingernail!

Poison dart frogs also use their colors to stay out of danger in their homes. Their beautiful, bright color combinations mean they are highly toxic. One kind of poison frog has enough poison in its skin to kill 10 human adults. Predators see the bright colors and avoid the frogs.

WORD WISE

A poison is a toxic material on an animal's body. A venom is a toxic material passed to other animals through a sting or bite.

The monarch's bright orange and black is easy to spot, but that is why the signal is effective. Some animals know it's best to leave the butterflies alone. Monarchs have a poison in them that comes from eating a plant called milkweed.

The bold yellow and black stripes on a bee also tell predators to leave them alone.

The bright colors scare predators away, as they've learned those colors could mean pain.

Some of the brightest colors can be found on the nudibranch, a soft sea slug. The bright colors work in two ways. They allow the animal to hide among the bright coral in the ocean. The colors also warn predators of its poisonous ooze. Nudibranchs eat poisonous animals. They can keep that poison in their bodies to use on predators.

Consider This

How did predators learn that bright colors mean to stay away from the animal with them?

Glossary

aggressive Ready or likely to attack.
alter To change.
behavior The way a person or animal acts.
bioluminescence The release of light from living organisms.
chemical Made inside of the body to help a living thing survive.
confuse To make someone not understand.
coral reef A structure in oceans that is formed by coral skeletons.
defend To protect oneself from an attack.
disguise To change the usual appearance in order to be unnoticed or unrecognized.
environment The surroundings a person, animal, or plant lives in.
larva A young often wormlike form (such as a grub or caterpillar) that hatches from the egg of many types of insects.
marine Of or relating to the sea.
nocturnal Active at night.
organism A living thing.
patient To be able to wait for longer amounts of time.
predator An animal that lives by killing and eating other animals.
prey An animal hunted or killed by another animal for food.
protect To keep safe from harm.
reflect To give back an image or likeness as if by a mirror.
register To acknowledge.
scales Thin, hard plates that cover the bodies of fish and snakes.
spine A structure made of bones, muscles, and other tissues.
texture The feel and appearance of the surface of something.
toxic A poisonous substance that could harm a living thing.
transparent Fine or sheer enough to be seen through.

For More Information

Books

Herrington, Lisa M. *Cool Camouflage*. New York, NY: Children's Press, 2018.

Jenkins, Steve, and Robin Page. *Look Again: Secrets of Animal Camouflage*. Boston, MA: Houghton Mifflin Harcourt, 2019.

Romero, Libby. *National Geographic Readers: Animals That Change Color.* Washington, D.C.: National Geographic Society, 2020.

Websites

A to Z Animals
a-z-animals.com
Read much more about all kinds of animals at this detailed website.

San Diego Zoo Wildlife Alliance
sandiegozoowildlifealliance.org
An international, nonprofit organization that strives to integrate wildlife health and care, science, and education to develop sustainable conservation solutions.

Publisher's note to educators and parents: Our editors have carefully reviewed these websites to ensure that they are suitable for students. Many websites change frequently, however, and we cannot guarantee that a site's future contents will continue to meet our high standards of quality and educational value. Be advised that students should be closely supervised whenever they access the internet.

Index